Raised to the Power of Love

Publisher's Notes

Raised to the Power of Love
© July 2016, Robin Chase, All Rights Reserved.
Published by Titan Book Publishing LLC
P. O. Box 112
Lake Wales, FL 33859-0112

ISBN 978-0-9830316-3-5

Raised to the Power of Love

A Collection of Poems

by Robin Chase

*To my parents
For all from each*

About the Author

Having a mother who creates art, and a father who teaches literature for a living and spouts Shakespeare at supper has an effect on a boy. So does listening in the pew of a church, while a grandfather's voluminous voice fills the air each Sunday. These things create a love of language and help to inspire a young man, who finds a symphony in the sound of the stories, a wonder in the words, and power in the pleasure of poetry.

That's how life was for Robin Chase as a child. At an early age, poetry was a part of everyday life; literature was everywhere, puns were sport, and oration was ordinary. The love of literature was in his DNA. At eight years old, he was writing poetry.

Raised to the Power of Love

When he was 18, he came to live with and care for Nelle, a blind woman 70 years his senior. When she was a young woman, Nelle had been married to Milton, who would read aloud to her and perform parlor poetry in their home for guests. She missed those bygone times and decided to groom and direct Robin in this old, and almost forgotten, art. The next year brought daily lessons in the delivery of a story or poem, how to enunciate each word, and to perform the work so to tell the story. She taught him the lost art of elocution. Robin treasured these times with Nelle, as she sculpted and crafted his naturally lovely speaking voice to her specifications.

Later, as a college student, Robin discovered the art of Readers' Theatre, and was further groomed by another older woman, Joan Lee, who nurtured him more, and instructed him in this new genre. She taught him to act the words, the importance of reciting, not reading, and how to feel the performance.

In the 21st century, it may not be the standard path for a poet to find his voice, but it's how Robin found his. His poems and recitations are from a time past, and the words themselves are directly from his heart. Maybe that's why his work and voice are so special and touching. They are the product of an aggregate of almost three hundred years of the experiences of his mentors and him. Robin's work is a result of their tending to, teaching, and caring for a young man, whom they felt was worthy of their time.

We, his audience, are the lucky recipients of their's and Robin's efforts. If you haven't yet had the opportunity to hear or read his words, you have a delightful treat before you with this book. And if you have had the pleasure of hearing him perform and recite poetry, this book will remind you just how much you enjoy it. Bonne lecture!

Table of Contents

About the Author vii

Raised to the Power of Love 1
Florescent Skunks 2
Novels 4
Reflections of Vincent 6
Our Rhododendron Day! 8
Silver Slivers 10
On the Point of A Needle 12
Shadow Flower 14
The Men of Set Design 15
A Jinks Toast 16
In this Camp They Call "Three Threes" 17
Clock Wise 19
To You Who Have Made Birds All of Your Life 21
Your Single Thread of Gold 24
This Daughter of Art 25
Our Sea Run 28
Postcard From Bohemia 30

Raised To the Power of Love

Today we have witnessed this problem you solved:
Given time is a finite amount,
And desires are countless for single days numbered—
For the hand of the one on whose hand you can count.

What is the formula for happiness?
Where does the true answer lie?
When is the solution?
Where is the proof?
And how do you solve for the who, how, and why?

So, you factor what's known and what's unknown.
You consider each logical sign.
Then you follow the steps to each other;
And you pair when the moment is prime,
As your distance breaks down to a point on a line,
Infinitesimally close in a fraction of time.

And you realize your absolute values.
And your hearts feel the run and the rise;
Till no sphere can eclipse the ellipse of your lips,
Or the slope of the curve of the love in your eyes.
And your halves make you whole.
And it's so much more so than the sum of such equal two parts.
Like a circle's perfection,
In every direction,
One ends where the other one starts.
For together as one you are greater than two,
For you've proven what few may know of—
Your love knows no limits,
Your hearts know no bounds;
You've been raised to the power of love.

Raised to the Power of Love

Florescent Skunks

Although you'd think you'd spot their stripes,
Not everyone may see, or smell, Florescent Skunks.
At least that is, not until the black light buzz goes on,
And their lines zig-zag distressed;
Then the wind blows your way only,
While they turn their tell tale tails,
Till all they leave behind shows acid glows;
Even in the presence of each incensed blossom rose.

And this is when one knows
That it takes more than just a nose for common scents
To realize the difference between what one sees as real,
And what is really there but is invisible.
For there is no reveal
until these coward friends have fled you,
Flowered child,
Lit black, how red.

You had let them come into your opened door at night
To table top perform;
Lick your bowl to satisfaction—
You allowed they clean your plate.
And then,
When reaching out to touch this hint
That that which once was wild you might now tame,
There was this switch they tripped on,
Charging your surreal fate—
An electric quick smile bite attack;
Slow low slinky peel away;
Your heart hold hand pulled back too late,
With the broken skin feel of betray;
The ultra violent white and black,

Robin Chase

And the spill of the bouquet.

But do not lash back at the traces
of those ghosts of yesterday—
What the back-flash flash-back back-lash is
Is hard for most to say.
And any tongue tied diatribe promotes what it debunks—
At one time and to someone
We've all been Fluorescent Skunks.

Raised to the Power of Love

Novels

We'd want to write novels,
All about our lives,
And lace the lines with pretty girls—
And housewives.
So when bookstores were deserted,
And libraries closed,
We patronized those places where the matron ladies posed
With their cigarettes and lighters,
And fixations for writers.

They'd say,
"Child, why you buying drinks for characters like me?"
—"I like pretty women.
And I'm almost twenty three."

They'd tell us what they're reading,
And we'd say we knew the author.
They'd want an introduction,
And we'd tell them, "It's no bother."
We'd tell them we were writers,
And they'd tell us they're impressed.
We'd want them in our novels,
So, we helped them get undressed.
We'd tell them what they'd want to hear,
"Yes, you're pretty Mrs. van Deveere,
It's all right, I'll turn out the light for you, my dear."

They'd talk about their love lives,
And so we'd sympathize.
They'd cry about their husbands,
And we'd apologize.
We never looked directly in their eyes

Robin Chase

When we flattered them with complicated lies;
When they'd cling to us like children,
And speak to us like spies;
When they'd fall asleep like twenty,
And wake up forty-five.
When we feared we left a footprint
When we stepped into their lives;
When we'd take them out to breakfast,
Like a consolation prize—
To their questions about books and alibis,
And our "Readers' Digest version" replies;
And our kisses for the last time,
And their "See you soon" good-byes.

Phone numbers on matchbook covers—
We were tired of those Saturday lovers.
We had to go to bed
And recover by ourselves.

They'd call us from their kitchens and bedrooms.
They'd send us silver pencils and pens.
We'd save them all for when we'd write our novels,
And we hoped we'd never hear from them again.
And we'd find excuses for Fridays,
And shy away from singles' dives.
And so we'd lie in bed and read our novels,
And dream about the novels of our lives.

Raised to the Power of Love

Reflections of Vincent
(In the Owl Room Mural)

The genesis is sketchy,
But conclusions can be drawn,
When this artist starts with nothing
But these walls to put it on.
He can trace it back from Adam to the eve of yesterday,
As the fruit tree of Creation
Has passed down her seeds his way;
There to germinate in genius,
Where those Sistine gardens grow—
In the essence of his senses,
Deep in shades of Michelangelo.

For it stems from roots in greatness
That he has risen to this height;
That from his earthen pallet
He has captured heaven's light,
And brushed upon a world that only few may understand,
As to his eyes and through his mind
Comes God's gift to his hand;
To coax forth strokes of brilliance
Across Time's endless span;
To hold a mirror up to life and touch the soul of man.

So thus, on close reflection,
There's so much more than meets the eyes,
As just beneath the surface a much clearer image lies;
You see, the mural of his story is—
His hand paints what his eyes see,
What his heart feels,
What his soul says.
So, mirrored on these walls in art,

Robin Chase

We see his mind, his soul, his heart,
We find Vincent Perez.

Raised to the Power of Love

Our Rhododendron Day!

It's Rhododendron Day!
It's Rhododendron Day!
Our Rhododendron Day!

—A day that one spends with one's friends,
Past where the road ends;
Where one comes to this Log by the Side of the Way,
And suddenly sees—
There are trees in these woods
That take pride they hide upright in shade.

But, let the sun shed some light;
They are less up tight,
And more in style,
Than you might first think.
See how they line the way today,
For our personal parade,
And together make their stands for the latest forest fashion.

It may be because by May
That they've had way too much to drink,
That with the greatest florists' passion
They decorate their feet,
With these trellis-trumpet blossoms
Of white, pink, and purple flowers,
To make their looks complete.

What was in those April showers
That such burly bodies preen?
—That some lean upon each other
Just to see and to be seen

Robin Chase

In Divine designer couture,
With each custom blossom bloom?
I hear the buzz among the bees is
Heaven sent perfume.
So I surmise...

Between the ascent and the descent,
To accentuate life's sweet scent,
Imposing redwoods put God's Spring line on display,
And accessorize,
Just for our eyes.
On Rhododendron Day,

It's Rhododendron Day!
It's Rhododendron Day!
Our Rhododendron Day!

Raised to the Power of Love

Silver Slivers

There is no horizon any more,
For most, I sense.
Now, nearly every view of worth
Is focused down at Earth
From captured, fractured, skies.

Before those highs were ever claimed,
That line between defined our way;
It was our fence against the prize
We knew we were not wise to know.
It told us where the unknown was,
And where we weren't allowed to go.

Now, higher than the tallest kings,
With shadows longer than their lands,
Some seek all secrets left above
The cover of the unseen things.
When once before,
A voice was held within the boundaries of the eyes;
Where no one's iris found the rings
Of halo circle sounds below,
With what machines' wings hear and show.

I whisper to the Sacred Star.
My sun defends the low and small.
I trust my moon.
In darkest times she'll shine her crescent glow for all.

False gods fall into crystal mirrors,
Preening to have cracked the code.
They cannot find this splintered skylight
Breaking through to blind their lens.

Robin Chase

They will not feel with shattered eyesight
Ancient Echo's silvan sounds.
Through these trees her treasures lie—
Night silhouettes,
Bright silver slivers,
Scattered pieces,
My twilight ground.

Raised to the Power of Love

On the Point of a Needle

Every scar is an unplanned tattoo
That the High-Seated Artist has penned upon you;
Who, with no inkling,
Sparkling, winking,
In the skin of perfection of a southwestern star,
Crossed into this parlor,
Searching for your sextant,
Drunken sailor from a bar.

How else to get "The Grand Design"—
Know that you are stellar and remarkable enough
To think that you could begin to plan it?
This voyage of yours,
In a body of water,
Porous, and rough, from the storm and the swell.
Now, you find yourself tossed off course, and sinking,
And signed in a barnacled shell.

Perhaps you forgot to chart how Mars felt,
When he awoke with a hangover shake,
Plotted and poked dragon red?
Know Venus chose "The Compass Rose"
As clothes for spotted marks,
Sunken by stones that were thrown from afar,
Though, she settled with anchors instead;
That the belts given Saturn,
Once bandaged and bleeding,
Are mermaids that circle a spar;
And Neptune wears Earthlings who breathe air where he is,
Beyond where those sliced vessels are.

Break through the surface, once again, lost sea men,
As first in your past as you flashed as the fastest of swimmers!

Robin Chase

Abandon the wreckage!
Turn on your backs and connect dots in darkness.
Above all then fathom—
How many life lines arrive on the point of a needle?

Raised to the Power of Love

Shadow Flower
(Jamuna II)

As heaven bends mid Summer sun to higher ends,
Here, on this Earth-skinned molten core,
That spins around her circle path;
There casts past shaded curves this bliss,
These fairy light spots in this forest;
As if to find each place to kiss—
The hidden secrets once in dark.

Shy shadow flower now revealed,
Rare beauty in these woods,
She sleeps.
So slight before the girth of trees,
This bright sprite at these birth of times.
Each instant more a dream awake,
As petals open up to light
The center of the universe she keeps.

Here in her sundial seconds,
She resets the galaxies,
While silence chimes her distant score
For waiting
Centuries.

Robin Chase

The Men of Set Design

To quote The Bard, who once the rage
Could fill a page for art,
"All the world is but a stage,
And each must play his part."
But where do players shake a spear?
Alas, for thee and thyne,
Who spins the Globe in seven days?
The Men of Set Design!

And in that week of work they take
They know to make a scene.
Their background is, for Nature's sake,
To grace her envy green.
For when a play is cast in stone,
Who quarries in a mine?
When men take wood for granite, praise
The Men of Set Design!

For it is when men's minds are set
That night might let dreams dawn
Where light and color both beget
What good men act upon.
So to these men whose work be play,
The play doth make them shine.
For no one paints the town red, like
The Men of Set Design!

Raised to the Power of Love

A Jinks Toast

I am a humble Jinkster,
Here with the best of Jinks.
I'm a little part of something great—
Like sphincter is to Sphynx.

Now the riddle is,
"What passes for a big hit or a flop?"
And when I'm working backstage,
Or under a backdrop,
I watch you "chew up scenery".
You digest each latest trend.
You're watching every movement,
And you see things to the end.

You know that what the outcome is
Is what goes into it.
Which goes to show that shows do go
'Cause Jinksters give a chit.
Our all consuming passion
Is what makes the most of art.
Its the sweet smell of excess
That sets us Jinkster men apart.
For we eat and drink the finest
Then cut loose with our instincts.

A toast to you,
And all you do!
To my good friends in Jinks!

Robin Chase

In This Camp They Call "Three Threes"

Come gather all you woodsmen,
And I'll tell to you the tale
Of this forest of redwood giants,
Left to guard this glen and dale;
About one gentle giant in this grove of memories,
Who, straight and tall, had grown to fall
For this camp they call "Three Threes."

He was made of toughest timber.
He was armed with thickest bark,
As alone he held the hillside,
At attention day and dark.
A sole and solemn sentry,
Here he stood for centuries;
Then came the day these woods gave way
To this camp they call "Three Threes."

At first he felt a campfire
Through a canopy of leaves.
Then he listened to the laughter,
And he eaves-dropped through the eaves.
Once, to test his heart, and hillside,
He leaned closer by degrees.
And so inclined he grew aligned
With this camp they call "Three Threes."

And as time marched he held his ground,
There on that canyon grade.
And for the men below,
He fought the sun, and won them shade.
Commanding morning stillness,
He could battle down a breeze;

Raised to the Power of Love

Hold up the sky, do or die,
For this camp they call "Three Threes."

The storm that laid him down
Was something only gods arrange.
He was knighted, first, by lightening,
Then cheered on by winds of change.
He was showered with affection,
And the thunder roared, "At ease."
And he let go at the get go
Towards this camp they call "Three Threes."

And in his first and final arc
He had one dream to keep.
He felt his limbs grow heavy,
And he slowly fell, asleep.
And through those eaves he'd eaves-dropped through,
He dropped through those eaves with ease;
And he came to rest, an honored guest,
In this camp they call "Three Threes."

Robin Chase

Clock Wise

I do not believe we've paid enough attention
To the contents of our times—
Those precious, precise, pieces,
Found beneath our scratched bezels and tarnished cases.

I say because, most lately, I have noticed up close,
There are these vast stretches of vacant spaces,
Where the faces of our clocks have not been etched,
Or scored.
Suddenly, I've become aware of the longest long lost places—
The escapements of far distant tics and tocs
That our carelessness has cursed
Because we chose to not take notice
Of each latest breath we took—
When we inhaled, and then released,
But not as if each life-filled second were adored enough
To fill a cared-for bubble to it's largest size.

When did you, and I, neglect to fully realize
Just how slowly "now" can happen
If our "then" is not rehearsed?
Or, if with our minutes then reversed,
When have we ignored how just how hastily they passed,
While we were so immersed in searching back
To where our early gears were stored,
We rarely watched years springs unwind,
Slow wasted as they went?

There is always a last moment before there is another first…
An away before there can be another toward;
And though fascination can become bored,
When even a bubble that carries our breathing

Raised to the Power of Love

Passes through air until shared care has burst,
As our glasses must be emptied
Before others may be poured,
This time, we must sip slowly—
Taste desires changing minds,
While satiation waits impatiently
For the next thirst on the dial
We will find, and fulfill.

From now on,
Let us become chronological—
Moving forward together with the big hand
With the little hand,
We will know no regrets when our balance wheel fails;
Till the spin of our movement no longer still tries.
When we breathe in to fill what will be our last
Most beautiful bubble,
We will know on our exhales
We had learned to live clock wise.

Robin Chase

To You Who Have Made Birds All of Your Life
(To Wheatley Allen)

You,
Who have made birds all of your life,
Must know what it feels like to yearn to fly.
How else then could you learn to make weightless wings,
With ease,
From weighted things?
Turn redwood trees to softest down?
Cast feathered promises in bronze, that song-bird-sings,
"Please wait for me!
I too will soar to my highest highs,
In my time.
I'm just waiting for the slightest breeze
To lift the lightest me
Straight up into my brightest skies!"

How is it you know birds so well
That you can make your Resting Quail
Trill and tell in quest filled songs
His longings to strum flight?

Come night,
When you nestle down to rest and your days eyes close,
Might you still so "moonward,"
Though inward then,
Past the shores of before fragrant Rosemary beds,
To where what boyhood driftwood knows,
You loon float,
As a sea gull slows,
You turn and migrate forward toward the steep,
The wide,

Raised to the Power of Love

The narrow—
There all too soon to eagle glide;
Free falling bird of prayer,
Descending dove man cupped in air;
Yet still then only half deep there
Into the vigilant sleep of the most fragile sparrow.

Here, does your mind leave the keep
Of the fingers and the hands of the heavier man behind
To hear the gentle call?
Is here where you know you can always go
Where you can look up and see the Blue Birds?

Will you follow them upwards then?
Through the hollow marrow of kindest tree trunks?
To emerge in their tall crowns of birch branches
With leaves that sway,
And there,
Flutter forward toward Creation's furthest light
Until you are where you are perched to leap,
At the furthest end of the bending when of go?

How else then could you know so perfectly
What grains of precious Wheat to leave,
What grains to feed to wind,
To nurture hungry birds in need of flight
From deepest wood,
And still weave your mate a nest
From hand carved shavings?

For you who have made birds all of your life,
Heaven's known where dreams crumbs lead;
How word by deed you've owned your sky.
Now birds eye views have shown your way;
Where you have found your faith to leap—

Robin Chase

Your gift to cross each rarest span;
Land on high church glass window sills,
To see through panes that lift a man
To where the birds of you have flown—
Into the warmth of the home of your Lord,
To fly on toward
Their daily bread from Jesus.

Raised to the Power of Love

Your Single Thread of Gold

There is more love within this room
Than any heart could ever hold;
For you have given each of us
An elemental part of you.
Like pieces of this family cloth,
Our lives are all connected
By your single thread of gold.

All without a book to go by,
All without a pattern near,
Seamlessly you've sown the seconds,
Matched the minutes,
Patched the hours.
You've mended days with perfect stitches;
Clothed our years in all your finest;
Closed the gaps to fight the cold.
You've held this family close together
With your single thread of gold.

Now we wrap our love around you.
For you have made this brilliant quilt.
Held together with your spirit,
Strong and endless,
Fine and gilt.
Now we blanket you with "Thank You."
Now you be warmed with truth be told—
Always we will all be strengthened
By your single thread of gold.

Robin Chase

This Daughter of Art
(To my mother)

Now time unveils a portrait
That the eyes have not yet heard;
An image that the ears have not yet seen;
Frames this canvas that stretches far past eight times ten,
Every year painted over and over again
With so many layers,
That barely the word
Can begin to describe
The true depth of her sheen.
Find her first past her last
Through the vast in-between.

From her very conception,
This daughter of Art so favors her father,
That she draws for him her first breath,
Then continues his line.
Not so much a reproduction
As an original work of Art,
Yet, of her own design.

As so you must know how she too is the daughter of
Mother of Pearl
Whose hues she exhibits early;
Here, colored akin
To the see through translucence in white-water-whirl,
Where sea-green and sea-blue seen only in sea
Swirl sunsets of coral and crimson within.
Here, she radiates outward;
Her light freed from prism where violet waves swell,
On the curl of a rainbow where visions begin,
Never ending whence seen.
Taste mixture,

Raised to the Power of Love

Sense texture,
Touch aquamarine.

Between vanishing points on her Zion horizon,
From one sight to the other.
A lifetime might dwell.
Here intricate brushstrokes
Chase heavens of dreams.
For forever views rest these peaks of her years.
Flowing consciousness streams
Feed her rivers with details,
Sorting shadows with sun gleams,
Down where near familiar trees
Pools spinning to twirl,
To wash past her roots,
Slipping back to beginnings,
All pieces together—
Quest worn,
Sifted well;
Last master mold shards from the cast of Art's girl,
Now as fine as his best clay
Poured once in a shell.

Here, at the base, near the edge of unpainted,
As chiseled in stone like his hammer stamp scrawl,
She makes a name for herself when she's finished,
Her cycle full circle she shows,
Claims her place,
With the mark that she made for all she created,
This daughter of Art Dallas Ball,
Dallas Chase.

Her morning,
Her afternoon,
Her evening hours,
Balanced on a wire,

Robin Chase

On a nail, on a wall.
Her landscapes alive,
Her still lifes still living;
Suspended in space,
Every moment still giving;
As if every day never ended,
At all.

Raised to the Power of Love

Our Sea Run
(To my father)

At first we walked on water,
Though, we did not even know it—
There was sunlight on the surface,
So we thought our path was golden.
Our footprints said, "we ran."
We left behind concentric circles,
That expanded ever wider.
We could not turn back to see.
We were quicker than the waves we left—
More buoyant than we weighed.
Our feet pressed to resistance,
With each greater stride we made.
We moved forward,
Ever fast, and unafraid.

No one said to us it was not so,
Nor that it could not be.
They may have from their shore,
But who could hear them anyway?
We were focused on our finish,
On the rhythm of our race—
On that our pace to close our distance could be true.
We never knew that some had drowned with weights
They placed upon themselves,
Although we listened once and noticed
Some who followed disappeared.
We thought they'd gotten tired,
And stepped aside to catch their breaths;
While we breathed into weightlessness.
Our bodies didn't exist.
We were effortless air movement,

Robin Chase

Fearless whirlwinds seeking sun.

We could not imagine stillness in our blissful, dangerous, way.
Our momentum couldn't trust resting,
Until we reached Earth again,
As the lightness we were given was withdrawn,
Pulled down toward shade.
In easy graduations,
We too became weakened, weary, and weighed—
Left windless, and breath-taken;
Beside ourselves,
On our shore,
Looking back at our sea,
Awash in waves that we had made.

Raised to the Power of Love

Postcard from Bohemia

Dear Friend,

Here is where I come to let my self mend.
There is music in this air.
Lo,
Higher notes than anywhere!
Though some were played four score ago,
They've still yet to descend.
But oh,
When I am here,
I swear I hear them sweet and clear;
And so my soul arises so,
In spires soars with those ago.
It's here I think of you and smile,
On how we'd spend a metered mile;
And I wish that you were here
To share this timeless symphony—
This gracious place,
Awhile,
With me.
I'll see you soon around the bend.
Let's keep in touch.
Let's stay apace…
It's by this way these woods are warm.

In friendship sound,

Robin Chase

www.ingramcontent.com/pod-product-compliance
Lightning Source LLC
Chambersburg PA
CBHW031507040426
42444CB00007B/1241